States
MAINE

by Angie Swanson

CAPSTONE PRESS
a capstone imprint

Next Page Books are published by Capstone Press,
1710 Roe Crest Drive, North Mankato, Minnesota 56003
www.mycapstone.com

Library of Congress Cataloging-in-Publication Data
Cataloging-in-publication information is on file with the Library of
Congress.
ISBN 978-1-5157-0406-5 (library binding)
ISBN 978-1-5157-0465-2 (paperback)
ISBN 978-1-5157-0517-8 (ebook PDF)

Editorial Credits
Jaclyn Jaycox, editor; Kazuko Collins and Katy LaVigne, designers;
Morgan Walters, media researcher; Laura Manthe, production specialist

Photo Credits
Capstone Press: Angie Gahler, map 4, 7; CriaImages.com: Jay
Robert Nash Collection, bottom 18; Getty Images: Heritage Images,
12, Portland Press Herald, 11, 29; Library of Congress: Prints and
Photographs Division Washington, D.C., 28; Newscom: Dennis Brack,
middle 18, ITAR-TASS, bottom 19; North Wind Picture Archives, 26,
27; One Mile Up, Inc., flag, seal 23; Shutterstock: Andrey Kozyntsev,
top right 20, cdrin, 6, Daniel Prudek, bottom right 20, dezi, top left 21,
Doug Lemke, bottom left 8, Everett Collection, 25, Featureflash, top 19,
hawkeye978, 9, hjochen, middle right 21, Jennifer A. Darrell, bottom
right 8, Jon Bilous, cover, 14, Joseph Sohm, 7, 16, Ken Wolter, top left
20, KWJPHOTOART, bottom right 21, Leonard Zhukovsky, 17, Maria
Dryfhout, bottom 24, marla dawn studio, top 24, Miriam Doerr, middle
left 21, Miro Vrlik Photography, 10, MVPhoto, bottom left 20, rasowit,
bottom left 21, s_bukley, top 18, spwidoff, 15, Steve Bower, top right 21,
Stocksnapper, middle 19, Zack Frank, 5, 13

All design elements by Shutterstock

Printed and bound in China.
0316/CA21600187
012016   009436F16

TABLE OF CONTENTS

Want to take your research further? Ask your librarian if your school subscribes to PebbleGo Next. If so, when you see this helpful symbol 🖱 throughout the book, log onto www.pebblegonext.com for bonus downloads and information.

LOCATION

Maine is the largest state in the northeastern region called New England. Maine is the only state in the country that borders only one other state. New Hampshire lies to the south and west. Canada wraps around Maine on the northwest, north, and northeast. The Atlantic Ocean lies to the east. Maine's capital, Augusta, is on the Kennebec River. The largest cities in Maine are Portland, Lewiston, and Bangor.

CANADA

N
W E
S

Legend
⚹ Capital
• City

MAINE

VERMONT

• Bangor

Augusta ⚹

• Bar Harbor

• Lewiston
Auburn

ATLANTIC OCEAN

Portland •

NEW
HAMPSHIRE

Kittery •

Scale
Miles
0   20   40   60
0   20   40   60
Kilometers

PebbleGo Next Bonus!
To print and label
your own map, go to
www.pebblegonext.com
and search keywords:

ME MAP

The North Maine Woods are a thinly populated region in the northern part of the state.

GEOGRAPHY

Maine has 3,478 miles (5,597 kilometers) of coastline. Many bays, harbors, and inlets add to the coastline. Farther inland, the coastal area is filled with marshes and tidal creeks. Acadia National Park is on Mount Desert Island and other small nearby islands. Visitors enjoy its rocky coastline, islands, mountains, forests, and lakes. The White Mountains of Maine are part of the Appalachian Mountains. Located in Baxter State Park, Mount Katahdin is the highest point in Maine. It rises 5,267 feet (1,605 meters) above sea level. Maine has more forestland than any other New England state. Forests cover 90 percent of the state.

PebbleGo Next Bonus!
To watch a video about the Moosehead Lake region, go to www.pebblegonext.com and search keywords:
ME VIDEO

Maine has many harbors, bays, coves, and inlets along its coastline.

Acadia National Park lies on the coast of the Atlantic Ocean in Maine.

Legend
- ▲ Highest Point
- Lake
- Mountain Range
- National Park
- River

Mount Katahdin

Moosehead Lake

Penobscot River

WHITE MOUNTAINS

Kennebec River

Acadia National Park

ATLANTIC OCEAN

Monhegan Island

Casco Bay

Scale
Miles
0   20   40   60
0   20   40   60
Kilometers

WEATHER

Maine's northern location keeps temperatures from getting too hot. Its average summer temperature is 64 degrees Fahrenheit (18 degrees Celsius). Maine's average winter temperature is 17°F (minus 8°C).

Average High and Low Temperatures (Augusta, ME)

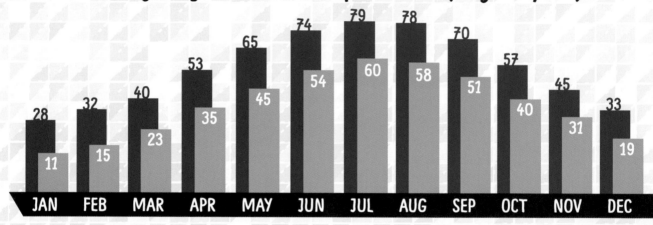

	JAN	FEB	MAR	APR	MAY	JUN	JUL	AUG	SEP	OCT	NOV	DEC
High	28	32	40	53	65	74	79	78	70	57	45	33
Low	11	15	23	35	45	54	60	58	51	40	31	19

LANDMARKS

Portland Head Light

Maine's oldest lighthouse, the Portland Head Light, was built on an order from George Washington in 1790. A museum there contains a number of lighthouse lenses and displays. Many other Maine lighthouses are also popular tourist spots.

Acadia National Park

Acadia National Park is on Mount Desert Island and other small nearby islands. The park was formed in 1919 and covers more than 47,000 acres (19,000 hectares). The park receives about 3 million visitors per year. Visitors enjoy its rocky coastline, islands, mountains, forests, and lakes.

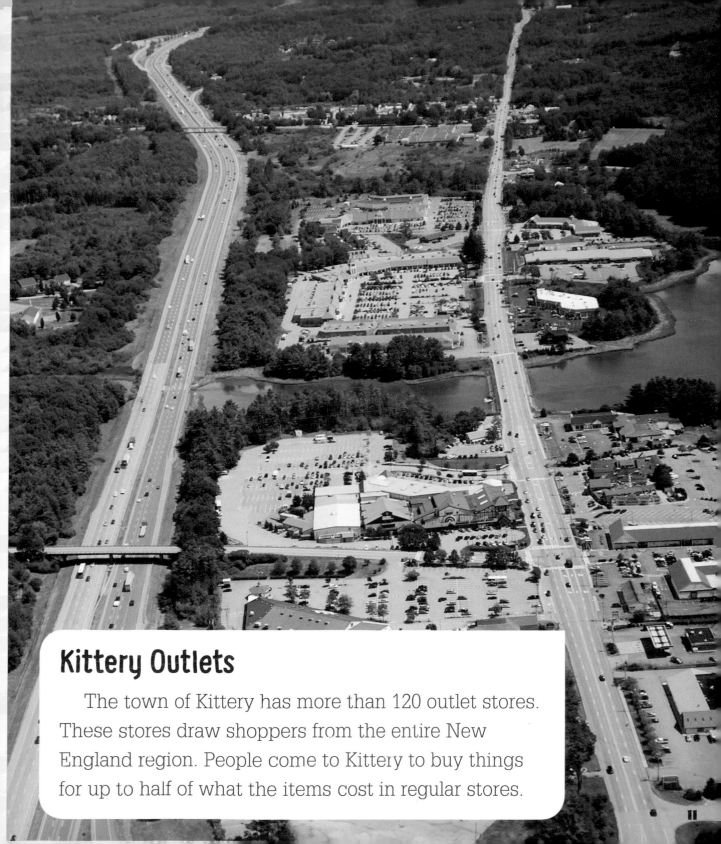

Kittery Outlets

The town of Kittery has more than 120 outlet stores. These stores draw shoppers from the entire New England region. People come to Kittery to buy things for up to half of what the items cost in regular stores.

INDUSTRY

Maine is the largest lobster-producing state in the country. Every year Maine harvests millions of pounds of lobster. Because of Maine's forests, the state produces many paper and wood products. Maine makes more toothpicks than any other state.

Because tourism is Maine's top industry, most towns have many shops. Kittery has more than 120 outlet stores that draw bargain hunters from all over the East Coast. L. L. Bean is a famous store founded in Freeport.

With about 17.6 million acres (7.1 million hectares) of forest covering the state, Maine's lumber industry is important to its economy.

Maine has a thriving agriculture industry. Maine produces 98 percent of the country's low-bush blueberries. Maine is the second-largest producer of maple syrup. Farmers in Aroostook County grow more than 2 billion pounds (907 million kilograms) of potatoes each year.

Maine has a large shipbuilding industry. The shipbuilding company Bath Iron Works is located in the city of Bath. The Kittery Navy Yard repairs nuclear-powered submarines.

Rare blue, yellow, red, and white lobsters have been discovered in Maine.

FAMOUS PEOPLE

Patrick Dempsey (1966–) was born in Lewiston and grew up in Buckfield. He starred in the TV series *Grey's Anatomy*.

Andrew Wyeth (1917–2009) was an artist who painted pictures of Maine's landscape and people. He was born in Pennsylvania and lived in Maine.

E. B. White (1899–1985) wrote books for adults and children. They include *Stuart Little* (1945) and *Charlotte's Web* (1952). He was born in New York and later lived in North Brooklin, Maine.

Stephen King (1947–) is one of the world's most famous authors of horror stories. He has written many novels that have been made into movies. He was born in Portland and graduated from the University of Maine.

Henry Wadsworth Longfellow (1807–1882) was a poet. His popular poems include "The Song of Hiawatha" (1855) and "The Courtship of Miles Standish" (1858). He was born in Portland and was educated at Bowdoin College.

Samantha Smith (1972–1985) wrote a letter to Soviet Premier Yuri Andropov in 1982 when she was 10 years old. The letter expressed her fears of a possible nuclear war between the United States and the Soviet Union. Andropov invited Smith to visit the Soviet Union, making her one of the country's youngest ambassadors for peace. She and her father were tragically killed in a plane crash in 1985. She lived in Manchester.

STATE SYMBOLS

Tree

eastern white pine

Flower

white pine cone and tassel

Bird

chickadee

Insect

honeybee

PebbleGo Next Bonus! To make a dessert using Maine's state berry, go to www.pebblegonext.com and search keywords: ME RECIPE

20

Cat

Maine coon cat

Animal

moose

Mineral

tourmaline

Herb

wintergreen

Fish

landlocked salmon

Berry

wild blueberry

1880s Bath Iron Works begins building steel ships. It's still a giant shipbuilding company today.

1948 Margaret Chase Smith of Skowhegan is elected to the U.S. Senate; she is the first woman to be elected to both houses of Congress.

1972 Edmund Muskie of Rumford runs for president of the United States.

1980 The U.S. government agrees to pay Maine's Passamaquoddy and Penobscot Indians for their seized lands.

1996 On September 27 an oil spill in Casco Bay causes millions of dollars in damage and harms the wildlife in the area.

1998 Independent governor Angus S. King is re-elected to a second four-year term in one of the largest margins of victory in Maine's history.

2012 On October 29 Hurricane Sandy hits Maine with winds of more than 60 miles (97 km) per hour and knocks out electricity to tens of thousands of homes.

2012 Maine lobstermen bring in a record 127.2 million pounds (57,697 metric tons) of lobster.

2015 Studies show the Gulf of Maine is warming rapidly.

Glossary

ancestor *(AN-sess-tur)*—a family member who lived a long time ago

commerce *(KOMM-urss)*—the buying and selling of things in order to make money

ethnicity *(ETH-niss-ih-tee)*—a group of people who share the same physical features, beliefs, and backgrounds

frontier *(fruhn-TIHR)*—the far edge of a settled area, where few people live

industry *(IN-duh-stree)*—a business which produces a product or provides a service

legislature *(LEJ-iss-lay-chur)*—a group of elected officials who have the power to make or change laws for a country or state

limestone *(LIME-stohn)*—hard rock formed from the remains of ancient sea creatures

marsh *(MARSH)*—an area of wet, low land usually covered in grasses and low plants

nuclear power *(NOO-klee-ur POW-er)*—power created by splitting atoms

region *(REE-juhn)*—a large area

sea level *(SEE LEV-uhl)*—the average level of the surface of the ocean, used as a starting point from which to measure the height or depth of any place

Read More

Ganeri, Anita. *United States of America: A Benjamin Blog and His Inquisitive Dog Guide.* Country Guides. Chicago: Heinemann Raintree, 2015.

Hicks, Terry Allan. *Maine.* It's My State! New York: Cavendish Square Publishing, 2015.

Wang, Andrea. *What's Great About Maine?* Our Great States. Minneapolis: Lerner Publications, 2015.

Internet Sites

FactHound offers a safe, fun way to find Internet sites related to this book. All of the sites on FactHound have been researched by our staff.

Here's all you do:

Visit *www.facthound.com*

Type in this code: 9781515704065

Super-cool **stuff!** Check out projects, games and lots more at **www.capstonekids.com**

Critical Thinking Using the Common Core

1. Name at least two types of food that farmers grow in Maine. (Key Ideas and Details)

2. Maine is famous for its lobster. Describe what you think it would be like to harvest lobster. Would you want to do that job? (Integration of Knowledge and Ideas)

3. What is the average low temperature in Augusta, Maine, for the month of May? Use the graph on page 8 to help you answer. (Craft and Structure)

Index